Chrysalis, Liberated

Natalie Aoife

BookLeaf
Publishing
India | USA | UK

Presentation by *BookLeaf Publishing*

Web: www.bookleafpub.com

E-mail: info@bookleafpub.com

ISBN: 9789357448970

First edition 2021

DEDICATION

To the family that I chose, this book is for you.

ACKNOWLEDGEMENT

To Shannon, Morgan, Annie, Laura, Andi, Amber, Catherine and Beth. May your inspiration be plenty, may your hearts be full, and your memories be eternal honey.

Thank you to Morgan Cooney (@commander_booty_call across social media) for the absolutely phenomenal book cover, which wouldn't have been realised without your skill and artistic prowess, and for being one of my all-time favourite artists.

PREFACE

This book is...a challenge. It's been challenging to not be entirely miserable in my writing, but, with COVID, the pandemic, and all that came with it, it's entirely difficult to not focus on the negative. A lot of good came of this year, and I'm glad I was so lucky. But it's hard to write joyous, ignorant nature poems when a lot of suffering has happened. A lot of change within myself too. Finally starting my transition, finally graduating (ish) from an undergrad and a postgrad degree. I've been incredibly lucky to write glorified emotional vent poetry. But, I hope someone reading this comes away feeling if not empathetic, at least understanding that mine is by no means the luckiest or the happiest COVID tale, but it's certainly a cross-section of some common experiences.

A Seattle Kiss At Dusk

The taste of vintage dust and fish-market
lunches hangs like a question on our lips
You promised me the moon and stars, and the
night air is crisp, clear, and your eyes sparkle.
Our hands have been entwined all day. I take joy
at the looks of passersby, you
baulk at the thought of being noticed. One of us
is a tourist in love, the other a maiden port.

The world doesn't exist except for the heat of
your soft body on mine. Your contours fill my
cracks
and you complete me. We are shapely together.
Nothing ordinary.
I wouldn't accuse you of such things. We're
some kind of hedron, one waltz from collision.
You call me honey, and the sweetness trickles in
the soft haze of summer heat on your pale skin.

I could promise whispers kept only for closed
doors, but I settle

 for a simple 'I love you'. The sea, laughter in
waves, takes care of the rest.
She's dark, but calm. You like to call me a
queen. I'm too modest for royalty.
We're here, and the night is its darkest. The
waves are a quiet, bubbled-up hiss
and you tell me to look in your eyes.

I see storms, and rocky shores, but beyond that,
mellow waters. Shallows.
A place to swim and lose the world. The ferris
wheel spins onerously behind us.
I reminisce on everything that came before this.
The heat, our sweat, your eyes.
A hand no doubt reaches, and I place it on my
wanting cheek.
Come lie with my bones, I offer. You chuckle
away the thought,
before I let you know how I feel.

The heat spins my mind for a record. A country
girl
used to living in much more frozen climes
clinging to animal furs
 and the fires of her enemies. I call myself a
bard, a storyteller
but your love, your kiss, the warmth of your
scarf wrapped around us both

you are my oral tradition to share around the campfire. If only to steal a moment of your time and know who we both were once, underneath the skins we wear.

Viking Funeral

The river is still in midwinter,
and the poppies yet to gleefully spring forth
the timber frets. It's not her time yet, her
latchings still young
tied to the grass of greener pastures. The snipes
gutter, circle
and descend on a helpless salmon. She does not
cry out of weakness
even as her eyes are pecked and her lifelines
plucked from her scales.

The raft bobs gentle-water
sundering waves battling for dominance
who can sink the body first?

Her eyes are full of stars that others have
plucked, returning them back
upon the astral canvas they believe she stole
from. Bandit fingers isolated
her nails stolen, leaving her without a scratch.

Her cold frame held hope, wind-chapped lips
still grasping whisper
hands roughened with time, effort. What was left
of blood, sweat and tears

mar the soft wool of her jherkin. Hastily pulled
over wool, her eyes blank
someone tried to steal her dreams. Her stiff
fingers, snake-coiled
never blessed with a lover's touch.

The gowns gather at the shore, fires in hand
vengeant Prometheus with a record to settle. If
she could see them,
their smiles a pantomine, she would cry. Friends
were the scars that meddle with her flesh
each flame a procession against their own
inward guilt. She was a no-one, she was always
a no-one.

If she could hear the crows circling as the flames
rose
she would smile, knowing she was returning
home.

Little White Pill

I feel like a fugitive, haunting the doorstep of
this muggy pharmacy
Egg-white walls and too-orderly shelves cast me
as a bandit escapist.
A woman throws her eyebrows. Antibiotics are
her hostage negotiation,
and this pharmacy is the wrong base of
operations.

The eyebrows hit the ceiling, I begin to collapse
under pressure.
Explaining multiple prescriptions for multiple
identities
as if the multitudes that live within me aren't
just the same depressed girl.
The sky threatens a rock festival, and I make the
mistake of leaving to the siren song.

I almost forget myself – a small bag doth butter
no parsnips,
and I accepted second prize (as if it would ever
be Vitamin D capsules)
I return, to the clerk's frustration, her dark
tresses ever-maddeningly spinning out.

She gives me a look as if she's due a
corporate-mandated aneurysm. I empathise, but
I know what I'm here for.

This has been a political machination a
half-decade in the making, I am Machiavelli
and these small, white pills are my sought
kingdom. For something so fragile,
so water soluble, to look at you brings me so
much joy. Two and a hundred miligrams of joy
in fact.
Estriadol, some fair maiden out of the greek
myths
that my mum used to read to me as a kid. Who
will she be? A great poet? A great author?

Or will she simply be happy? Knowing that the
woman she was born to be
is finally, finally, finally within her reach.

Chosen Name

Names – fleeing from a tactile legacy
hunted snakes praying gestate
land spirits toe a fickle line
under the guise of public enemy

old kings of the celtic lands,
old titles, a full syringe of memories
as the standing stones come crashing down.

I stand like a dolman, awaiting the next time
my chosen name is dashed upon the stones
where the legacy of a king, the king once forged
remains the subtle knife among the ashy rubble.

I call myself an outcast, bent on removing
apparatus
heart-beaker overflowing with hydrogen
waiting to pop at any minute. It's a test of my
fortitude
balancing expectations and a membership to an
identity
sand, slipping through my fingers

topple, circle the drain
trickle down the river.

The crows can eye the descent of nameless
things
beaded suspicion, before tearing apart a feral cat

it's a ritual of spite
and the cat's eyes glow in starlight.

Blink and You'll Miss Her

I saw you blink when I told you my name / my
true name
you offered tears / hopeless swells on cold
hardwood
are you sure? / is this what you want? / I love the
old you
catch the look before it disappears / a firefly flits
in dim rooms
a dim warmth against the winter winds of your
distant shoulders

Floating Somewhere, Michigan Summer

I think about us floating in a pool somewhere
It's the dead of summer, the heat is sticky on our
tongues
Your wife hangs out under a parasol, no doubt
drawing tablet in hand
Geese would come up naturally in conversation
To be honest, geese were always the
conversation
We're floating on rubber rings, adrift from the
world
The incandescent light cicada hiss dribbles
Trickles god-rays on our hooves. White girl
sunburn
and hopeless attempts to quench a hunger for
Faygo

You have dreams, maybe you've accomplished
them
reaching for the soft, June-thunderclouds that
threaten a good time

Maybe I brought my own wife along for the trip.
Maybe you love her
and maybe we're all getting along. Someone's
brought an order of sushi, and you always
promised you'd take me
so maybe salmon is poetic justice after all.
Maybe we're all happy
All adults, all accomplished, all living lives
Maybe is the rim-shot on the otherwise sterling
drum performance
I no doubt try to give.

Do we have our own kids? Are they running
around? The wind's rustles are louder now, and
your wife tells everyone to come inside
and suddenly I'm alone again. It's August, it's
muggy, and I'm isolated.
And I miss you, and I'm trying to say sorry,
but the words boiling my throat are ones you've
already forgiven

Maybe future us have the answers,
but being trapped in blue-sky brick cobble did
no one any good
least of all the family we make. I want you to
open the door,
but someone else has the key, and we can't
exactly ask him.
You don't make promises you can't keep,

and I don't think small dreams. Maybe if we'd met earlier
today's story would be different. I don't know if it would be better
but I'm afraid of the alternative. I worry about drifting out to sea
worried that no one would catch me. I know your fears are similar
scared of sinking into the mud when the beautiful night sky
twinkles moonbeam trickles on the darling ocean

You're a star, and I'm a tsunami, both waiting to collapse
maybe you can share some of your light with me one day.

To A Younger Me

Dear younger me,
it gets easier. It's a cliché. But it's useful.
You're getting bullied for being different. Never
mind differently abled.
Mum and dad aren't listening.
They aren't now, but things line up so that one
day they will.
You beat yourself up so He doesn't have to.
Break the metaphorical bone so walking limp
means he may lay off his assault for the day. It
doesn't work.

You come out of grammar school hospitalised,
humbled, harrowed.
H words. Hatred. You learn the meaning of
hatred. It sticks by you.
Its sticky claws, oozing oily words of revenge in
your ears. I know you try to listen
and fail because something stops you.
Loneliness, langurous and lingering as it is
doesn't last. You'll fail your A-Levels. I'm sorry,
I'm going to rip the plaster off now.
But it doesn't mean you're a failure. You
actually come out of failure with a smile of relief

and it tastes weird. Happiness still does. There,
another H word.

Happiness. Mum and dad may close that
disappointed bedroom door,
dooming you in the abject quiet of your own
vortex brain patter. But you do get what you
want.
Keep an eye out for the crows this time, for me.
Three crows means you're in safe hands.
I know it's weird. Trust me though. You're going
to start a new time in your life.
Heck, you're getting a girlfriend. I can hear you
doubting me through the page.
You can doubt me all you want, but cherish her,
alright? Life's going to get crazy.

While you're hiding from the world outside that
cul-de-sac we hated so much, you find a new
one
and you get to pretend to be whoever you want
to be. You try out being a knight, a storyteller
but you settle on being called "Natalie." I know
this sounds weird, but it's the truth.
You realise
after years of scar subtlety and brain-bashing
badness that you're actually a badass.
A woman. She's called Natalie.

You love Xmas. You love that feeling of
togetherness. Why not celebrate your love for
others
with a deep, unrepentant (and sometimes
completely batshit) love for yourself?

It's going to take a while. University (and yes,
you do go to university) is going to be a
wake-up call. You'll get lost in the woods and
with a vivacious, full body, victorious battle-cry
in the welsh wilderness, you'll find two other
weirdos to share your heart with. Then another,
and another.
You'll be called a sister, instead of a failure. It'll
feel nice. You'll fall into love, then out of an
abusive relationship. But it'll teach you a lesson
you needed to learn.

I love you, you dope. So that means you'll learn
to love yourself.

Dear younger me, it gets easier.
We're in a pandemic now. Things are confusing
again.
Maybe in six years, I'll write another poem like
this to another me.
Maybe we'll discuss who we used to be over
coffee, all three of us,

Maybe I'll see you flourish in the future, just as
you're starting to flourish now.
Your friends believe in you. Your chosen family
does too.

You chose your family, your friends. And now,
you get to choose your happiness.

Run towards the horizon with that flame,
however small it is.
And by all the gods in all the realms, don't let
anyone catch you.

Hallmark

I have fantasies about smoking
knowing it wouldn't leave me morning-aftered
with much more than lung cancer
it's the 4am Hallmark movie bliss
frustrated protagonising, agonising
over the Jennifer Anniston lookalike

The rain falls in sleek street sheet streaks
Some people call it the Coming of Christ
The tobacco-warmth filled the wanton hole
where the rain got in

it's having fantasies of release from inward pain
exhaling all the black mould of my lungs
coughing out a self-help storm
 the cold is agony
I don't wear gloves, entrapped in finger prisons
some kind of Christ can't stop me

my alveoli are kelp tugging weight
gulping hungrily for some sustaining storm
a seabed Nile-dried, lost its name to corporation
you can't make a movie about the seabed

the roots of my gnarled fingers, ripe for the
drop-off
I stopped worshipping the grind
when storms and death came kin to my door
old friends, darkening the kaleidoscope
of my ever-shrinking horizon

we're all broken lighting fixtures training our
colours on some
ancient, liver-spotted got-here-by-nepotism
actress
tangled in the mosswebs of some self-imagined
hate nirvana
some fish peck at my dulling irises, sparkling
celtic blues
just like the rains from back home

when you first told me you were proud of me

Traversing the Keyhole

Tiny paw whittle-whispers
onlookers snout, the whisker world
the world of Tall Ones is a world of worries.

We know not of the disease of the Tall Ones.
They collapse and cajole above us, offering us
their bodies
as we feed on their perished, timeless bones. Our
pups go strong
as the Tall Ones collapse, one by one, like their
dominoes.

Our world is next-day's food, the wet-damp
alley
and the inevitable hunter's trap. The Tall Ones
find us, if their mercy is barren
we become their sport when other prey be too
mighty to hunt.

We are communers-in-fleas, forgotten in
derelicts

and pothole sanctuaries. They cough and wince only to collapse
like mighty oaks, one foot in the grave, and one hand on the bedside.

The world above us is a world we see, but do not know
where the Tall Ones live and die, and where we will never go.

Scrying Lightning

When the wisp-flicker trickled, smoke tickles
the darkness was a thick, matte weave around
the candle
her heat and light a terminus for harmful
thought.

Surrounded by a bowl, the ocean draws in the
worst
the mind could hiss. The poisons, the failures,
and the anger of mankind
distilled into floating islands, stormy seas and
flammable whispers.

The sea-salt wind exhales in steady gasps,
releasing kelp from the lungs
and seawater from her bones. She is the daughter
of oceans, seabirds
and unhealthy amounts of wanderlust.
Cram-packed into terraced mazes
crumbling post-popular wartime bricks, making
a home for herself in fire
and in self-questioning.

Delve into the infinite, pull at the kelp-strings of
fate

twist and snip the chaff, until the blemishes
bevel. Until you become one
with your truth.

She was never male. The whirlpool cascades the
empty, useless thoughts
filling her mouth with fire. She breaths new life
into the empty sea, gifts it fauna
as she realises her truth. Burns away the old, the
islands that no longer buckle to her storm path

She is the hurricane, erasing the old and the dead
allowing for the seeds of something better to
sprout
the winds of change, be mighty fierce
obliterating all of the coast to make way for
calmer seas.

End of the Line

It's finally the end of the line
I should be thrilled - instead I'm spun wondering
/ webbed / why?

Everything's open, and everyone's pleased
as peas / as punch / as riots in the streets
to run amok / to frolic free again
no one to tell us what to do

Freedom to touch / to feel / to hate
for pleasure / for pain / for personal gain
it's time to escape / eclipse / evolve
from this sorry state of conservative affairs

What is freedom —
but freedom for everyone?
Freedom to kill, freedom to harm
Freedom to choose the woes
to inflict on those less fortunate?

It's the end of the line, the death of the old
the birth of the new / the fires of the lost
What's the cost of freedom?

Tarantula Hawk,
Wasp Nest

Crack the skull-firkin / the last days of life
socket nostalgia and dusty memories. Ambling
clambering from the shell of dead names,
feeding
seducing the truth-meat, the queen erupted from
egg-fervour
jellied in her womanhood.

Wasp pup rises from the primordial ooze. Tastes
the air, every blooded scent
every memory of the egg she used to wear,
 queen wasp draped in eggshell, coronated.

She is the queen of her jellied domain. Viscera
monarch
her court is corpse, her rule is undergrowth. She
is chattered whispers
of a new self borne from devouring the old. The
femur-flute sings,
whistles and throttles at the notion of her
presence.

She awakens from skeletal gestation, birthed
into a world of order
a wasp queen, tasting the inferno of her
ash-filled nest.

A world of control, decisions
and her decision is to exist.

Chemical

Self-replicated illness, caught in the drawstring
We observe the glowing weather
from the paranoia of week-old bedsheets.

Distraction is our vaccine,
injecting ourselves with daytime.
Watching greener pastures bliss, with awe.

A kingdom of deadened silence,
albeit for the bleat of ignorant lambs. Too young
to know different
than a holiday for viruses.

We mourn for the living behind riot shields
each wistful park footprint a criminal
thumb-mark
on a child's spotless bill of health.

Each abated disaster
caught live, the screen's corruption.

Be safe in your homes, they said.

Watch, as the sun sets.
On us, on them

on everything and forever.

Finale

I wish our hands could touch again
melting like they used to on warm summer
evenings
where the quiet was simple and still.

We're tired now.
Watching the sunset bleed into tabloid print,
its spinning grave the reputations scattered
ashes into the sea.

The day bruises into purple scars
Mother Earth heals
But is she safe when no one hears her whisper?

I long for a still night,
Blessed by the buzz of fluorescence.
The sparks dancing quiet down the empty street
so as not to disturb sleeping children.

Sometimes
I miss the "you" that I used to be.
Unhappiness was a simple matter
where I wasn't trying hard enough.

Watch the birds soar, in their fledgling nests.

Slipstream monarchs, their beautiful waltz
twirling, endlessly, into the knitted darkness.

Special Interests

Dopamine.
Eyes pulsate — glee's the word.
She, the archaeologist
digs through the small words
and bones of conversation.

Each inkling phrase is a seedling world
fresh with electric excitements. A dance of
stumbling
and follow-through. Some call it a fool's errand

Some call it obsession. You call it hobbies,
interests,
small worlds to pass time. She watches, aloof to
your childlike wonder,
As if the simplicity of your machinations breaks
coldly
against the frozen shore of her concern.

Your pen-grip is aloof, loose.
Each brush stroke of her denial aches,
raising your charcoal dagger
to the throat of a scorned god.

Patient Fertiliser

I want to save you, a nurturing motherhood
feckless, careless — you could've been beautiful
but instead, a rose inhales pesticide to spite the
weeds.

As dawn breaks against terracotta-potted shores
she reverses this tide of thorns, a terracotta
terror.
Rose, rise above the garden.

We are nothing but patient fertiliser.

You are broken.
An irreparable crack — why fix the stakes?
This game of pawns has been rigged from the
start.
Egg splatters, she wears her thankless yolk as
war paint
boxing against the endless shadows of foxes,
hawks
and television static.

Floating

I want to float.
I want to feel that feeling of anywhere else
between my toes
watching the tide drench the neon signs of a new
found family
exfoliating roots of poison.

I want the dark of night to kaleidoscope
on beckoning, walk the boards of tragedy
like a constellation of toggles, knobs and
regretful twists
each dream pre-plucked, pre-packaged, and
marketed for taking.

Anywhere else is too soon, and any other time is
too far away
terraced sand trickle-fingered and confusing the
lacing
tickled pink the sensitive bud subject. As if her
space clittered with noise
gendered her into trash sprawl. A bin panda, if
you will, burying its dead.

Dysphoria, a calling card. Living just under the
sewage crust

when the tax man arrives to starve your efforts.
Be the perfect son by morning
as if the banshee's claw-aching existed no more
in sound than in the death of silence.

If my world was an ocean, with obsidian depths
and pre-histories waiting to enact bloody
violence
perpetrate my skull as a nesting place for
revenge long since given the vocabulary to
alight
I would float, seperating the flesh
from the inky, sleepless darkness.

"Happy" Poem

I've been asked to write a happy poem
as many times as I've had fingers and toes.
Obfuscate the truth in smoke and mirrors,
Pierrot makeup dashed funhouse-style
and served sunny-side-up.

Capture a fleeting camera shutter
of a moment, in all its many trappings
lacing, composition and frilled to filling.

A sad movie without tears
is a dessert without substance. There is no storm
without rain
or thunder. There is no struggle without war, a
winner, and a defeated obstacle.

I am no comedy, nor is my life tragic
I am a daughter of crows and inclement weather
rising the thermals, in search of lightning
to dress feathers and parley with my enemies.

A happy poem is a measure of everything in a
life
the good and the bad together, mixed in
bittersweet symphony

a recording of a moment,
a second captured in a teardrop.

Heaney on the Pew

Liverpool, she shines. The old church hangs
quiet
and she, the breathing city, mourns the passerby.
We used to read her myths together, before bed.
You filled my heart with stories, and dreams
like Eucharist for the taking.

Nature is a social fiend. Her lessons were
half-baked stones, and the sparkle in my
childhood was fresh
water-rounded, ready to skip along the lake.
You garden now, with worn hands. Tender from
pain
fate had no right to bestow. Provision was your
gift
and I was reminded if I deserved such grace.

The stain-glass facades kept the sunbeams away
Stunted the phosphorescent fungus from
enveloping
the untouched church, and all her pristine
beauties.

We bonded over nature. Human, animal, it was
all lessons learned

and frustrations teethed out into quiet isolation.
Schools were trenches, and I was your unwilling
patriot.
No sooner a corpse than a paratrooper from the
troubled days.

Heaney was a church boy.
Following, dutiful in line to the drills of spuds.
Yours was an effort
twenty three years in the making. Little Seamus
kept us afloat
a mother otter steering her broken pup to shore.

There was no kelp to shelve what I became.
Judgement
was a livestock affair. Brother took up the arms
left by the soldiers
and I retreated into words when I could not
defend myself.
He became the family's everything, when I came
out broken.

There was no glue factory that could take me
so I wobbled, freshly jellied. Free to a harsh
world
for broken fillies were never meant to trot so
fierce.

Dark thickets were a campground for loose
thoughts
piled together like the aluminium taste
of kerosene-coddled sausages in a can. The
hunger,
oncoming thunder and her misty tongue
trickled us like tributaries. A taste for karaoke
and a fear for striking lightning. Rose-tinted
childhood
Addled flavours of happier memory.

I remember those words old man Heaney spoke
that coloured my taste for family. I'd have no
spade to follow men like my father.
Maybe if I keep digging, the family grave will
shallow
and so to will the guilt of being born a son.

Denial Is Not A Creative Colour

Autumn christens Ullet Road, baptised
in an orange glow. The daytime commute
she roars, dominant concrete bubbling lips. She
spits out twigs and
I wig out spinning   a drag yarn,
creative.

My writing feels like poison cloth
bandit digits twitch   vixen, outfoxed
the grand old duke of York avenue
had his ten thousand   dead

roots gnarled by time,   she cries
you're our son. churches loom
I can still smell   burning witches
crispy, bubbled-tongued
 rebellion

how long can you pretend to be a hero
as you   gently
snuff   your child down to sleep

feel-hands   creep, cup my breasts
announce   my plastic intentions
Stub my mind with cigarette doubt
just like our   dying ancestors
choking from blight,   you smile
your pelt is   a royalist gold.

manicured streets
    manicured middle-class
rebellion quashed dripping mouth
suckle mead grope a barmaid
cosplay anarchist.

we can all be   creative

Pink Sweater

I used to hate you. You made me feel overweight
burdened by chains and dragged under the reeds.
I was adrift,
askance from who I thought I was. You floated
away from me
gloating your fabric superiority. Your sleeves hid
my arms,
we shared a creed of secrecy. You kept me hush.
I was shapeless.
I'm not sure where we got you from, or whether
I tracked you in
but I took you back after she left. I tried to
reclaim you. Wash her smell off you
gently nurture the body underneath. Keep her
warm, but remind her of the soothing breeze.
I found it easy to discard what I couldn't burn
away. I kept you though.
Like you were the first thing I ever owned. A
ratty sweater that told the world "this is me."

I'd never owned anything like you before. I
think about ownership, and how I always
belonged
to others, and never the self I was building
alone. The she I was meant to be, after all. I was

your sweet mannequin, dolled up and ready to
be ravaged by a hungry audience.

Then she came. A storm out to artificial sea. But
I only wanted to see her eyes,
not the maelstrom of teeth and gilded lies she
desecrated in her wake. My landscape was
scathed,
bordered and hidden. If I gazed hard enough into
the misty bay, I can still feel the scar.
No one else notices. I did a good job of
rebuilding the coastline after the storm tore it
apart.

So you lay discarded. We lay discarded together.
Being discarded felt peaceful.
We got washed together, took care of each other.
But when I realised you were comfortable,
we rested together.

Maybe one day, I'll pass you around a campfire.
Or to a next of kin.
You'll be altered, taken in, sorted out. Chunks
removed, imperfections blemished.
Bevelled, curved and served on a catwalk platter
just like you always dreamed.
Tickled pink like the wool of what we used to
knit together. The stories.

We can make sure the last story ends on a high
note.

44